THROUGH THE LOOKING GLASS

"Through the Looking Glass" reveals the fragile boundary between myth and reality, guiding readers on an immersive journey into the world of myths' resonance in modern life. Blending ancient science with modern fiction, inviting readers to question what they see, and encouraging them to discover the truth hidden in myth and legend woven into reality Dive into a realm of timeless mystery, where the line between fact and fiction blurs, forcing you to reconsider your understanding of reality.

Let me know if you want this done or have specifics in mind!

Myths

Dear Reader,

Thank you so much for choosing to purchase this book. I sincerely hope that it enriches your knowledge and inspires you to delve deeper into the world of myth. It has been a labour of love, and I truly appreciate your time and effort in exploring its pages.

If you found this book valuable, I would be deeply grateful if you could leave a review on Amazon. Your kind words and thoughtful feedback not only encourage me but also help guide my journey as an author, ensuring I can continue to bring meaningful content to readers like you.

Thank you for your support, and I look forward to sharing more adventures with you in the future.

Warm regards,

Eti

<u>index</u>

Chapter 1: Why Myths Matter: Understanding the power of myths and legends and why they persist.
Chapter 2: The Science of Myth-Busting: A brief look at the process of debunking myths, from research methods to expert perspectives.

Part I: Historical Myths

Chapter 3: The Lost City of Atlantis
Myth vs. Evidence: Plato's Atlantis and various archaeological findings.
Chapter 4: Cleopatra, Queen of the Nile
Separating the myth of Cleopatra as a "femme fatale" from the historical ruler.
Chapter 5: The Trojan War
Myth vs. reality in the stories of Homer's Iliad and recent archaeological discoveries.
Chapter 6: Ancient Wonders and Mysteries
The Pyramids, Stonehenge, and other monumental myths.

Part II: Myths in Science

Chapter 7: The 10% Brain Myth
Unpacking the myth of limited brain usage and insights from neuroscience.
Chapter 8: Evolutionary Myths
Misconceptions about human evolution, "missing links," and Darwin's theories.
Chapter 9: Space and the Moon Landing Hoax
Addressing conspiracy theories about space exploration and the 1969 moon landing.
Chapter 10: Common Misunderstandings in Physics
Separating fact from fiction about black holes, parallel universes, and other space phenomena.

Part III: Myths in Medicine and Health

Chapter 11: Ancient Healing Myths
A look at ancient remedies and whether they work, from acupuncture to Ayurvedic practices.
Chapter 12: Health Myths that Persist Today
"You need eight glasses of water a day," "cold weather causes colds," and more.
Chapter 13: Alternative Medicine vs. Science
The myths surrounding homeopathy, detoxes, and miracle cures.
Chapter 14: Fitness Myths
"No pain, no gain," "spot reduction works," and other fitness misconceptions.

Part IV: Natural World Myths

Chapter 15: Animal Myths
Myths about wolves, bats, snakes, and other animals.
Chapter 16: Forest and Mountain Myths
Tales of the Yeti, Bigfoot, and other mythical creatures of the wild.
Chapter 17: Ocean Myths
Exploring mermaids, the Kraken, and other oceanic legends.
Chapter 18: Weather Myths

"Lightning never strikes the same place twice" and other weather beliefs.

Part V: Cultural and Religious Myths

Chapter 19: Karma, Luck, and Superstitions
A look at the origins and impact of beliefs in karma, luck, curses, and blessings.

Chapter 20: Sacred Sites and Their Stories
Myths around famous spiritual sites, like Lourdes, Mecca, and Bodh Gaya.
Chapter 21: Religious Legends
The reality behind stories from religious texts, such as Noah's Ark, the Exodus, and others.
Chapter 22: Festivals and Their Mythical Origins
Exploring myths and stories behind holidays like Halloween, Christmas, Diwali, and more.

Part VI: Technology and Modern Myths

Chapter 23: Technology Myths
Misconceptions about AI, computers, and hacking.
Chapter 24: Urban Legends in the Digital Age
The spread of urban legends on social media and how they impact society.
Chapter 25: Conspiracy Theories
Myths and misinformation around famous events like 9/11, Area 51, and the Illuminate.

Conclusion

Chapter 26: Why We Need Myths and Why We Need Facts
Exploring the balance between myth, belief, and scientific fact.
Chapter 27: The Future of Myths
How myths evolve and what future myths might look like in a rapidly changing world.

Introduction

The introduction aims to set the stage for the reader by explaining why ancient and modern myths hold significant cultural and psychological power. Provide a brief overview of what the book will explore, and comment on the persistence of myths and stories in human life, their psychological functions, and their role in shaping our beliefs, practices, and the world a we are in the middle of it

The introduction should prompt the central question of the book: Why do we continue to believe in myths even when evidence and reason seem to contradict us?

…………… so far .

Chapter 1: Why Myths Matter

Overview:

This chapter aims to show the importance of myths and legends in human history and culture, shed light on the universal life of all societies Purpose: the reasons for the existence of myths, its ideology, life of cultural activities, why we continue to tell these stories in the face of modern knowledge and advances in science1.1 Universal mythology

Mythology has been present in every culture throughout human history, from the ancient myths of Greece and Rome to aboriginal creation stories and modern pop culture myths in this section you can find the following.

• The role of myth in early human life: How ancient cultures used myth to explain natural phenomena (e.g., thunder as the voice of the gods), human life, and moral behaviour.

• Folklore as cultural memory: Folklore often tells the story of a nation's shared history and values, helping to preserve traditions, shared experiences and wisdom for generations

• Psychological needs of myths: Using psychology, myths can be seen as narratives that satisfy a deep human need for meaning, identity and connection to something larger than oneself role.

1.2 Myth and folklore

This section will examine the psychological reasons why myths are so compelling and enduring. Explore theories from psychology and sociology to explain why myths appeal to people in different times and cultures:

• Previous images of Carl Jung: Jung argued that some myths and symbols resonate universally because they tap into a "common unconscious" — shared symbols and experiences of all people — e.g.

• Joseph Campbell's One Track: Campbell's view of the hero's journey shows how myths universally follow a narrative that reflects human growth and experience, creating a timeless appeal.

• Emotional power of information: Humans are naturally attracted to information because it stimulates emotions, helps us make sense of our world, and offers ways to understand and deal with the uncertainties of life.

1.3 The persistence of myth in the modern era

Even in today's scientifically advanced world, myths grow in both traditional and new forms. In this section you can see:

• Contemporary Myth and Urban Narrative: How myth adapts to contemporary concerns such as "post-assassin" myths or urban narratives of horrific objects or events.

• Myths in Popular Culture: How Myths Reappear in Movies, Books, and Television. Examples might include the persistence of superhero stories, the use of mythological elements in fantasy literature (e.g. Tolkien's use of mythology), or conspiracies such as the "moon landing conspiracy". to be established.

• The enduring importance of myths: Regardless of scientific justification, people rely on myths for comfort, meaning and identity in times of uncertainty. Myths help people explain complex events or phenomena that may seem beyond understanding or control.

Chapter 2: The Science of Mythology

Overview:

The goal of this chapter is to provide the reader with an understanding of how myths are debunked or demystified through the use of scientific methods, research, and critical thinking. You will be introduced to the tools of myth busting, from historical and empirical analysis of myths, to how experts use logic, evidence and scepticism to disprove long-held beliefs

2.1 What is myth-busting?

Start by defining "myth-busting" — the practice of thoroughly or critically examining myths, legends, and false beliefs using the scientific method and thoughtful information: It involves:

• Distinct facts in fiction: how stories are often based on partial, misinterpreted, or pure truths, and how investigators work to discover facts.

• Critical thinking and skepticism: It is important to question assumptions, challenge unprovable claims, and view evidence objectively. Introduce the scientific method as a way to test myths (e.g., hypothesis testing, observation, peer review).

• Role of experts: It is important to consult reliable sources such as historians, scientists and subject matter experts to bust myth

2.2 Methods of myth breaking

This section will discuss some specific methods and techniques for debunking myths:

• Research and data collection: Discuss the importance of rigorous research in busting myths. This can include historical records, archaeological evidence, and modern technologies such as carbon dating or forensic analysis.

• Testing and empirical testing: Myths can sometimes be tested through experiments or controlled surveys. For example, urban myths, such as the myth that coins thrown from a large height can be fatal, can be scientifically verified.

• References and peer review: The scientific community often relies on peer-reviewed publications and references in academic disciplines to provide information that challenges myths. This is especially important when tales cross fields such as history, biology, and psychology.

• Fact-finding and misinformation prevention: Modern tools such as fact-finding organizations and online forums are part of the myth busting process, especially when it comes to myths and conspiracy theories using social media the.

2.3 Expert opinion on falsifying myths

In this section you can delve into how experts in various fields approach the task of busting myths:

• Historians: Historians trace the origins of myths and show how they develop over time. For example, an examination of the "flat earth" myth and its persistence despite overwhelming evidence to the contrary.

• Anthropologists: Anthropologists study myths in different cultures to understand its origin and function. For example, the mythology of a particular culture is analysed to determine how it reflects social structures or human behaviour.

• Scientists: Scientists often debunk myths about the natural world. You can use examples like the myth that vaccines cause autism or the myth that humans only use 10% of their brains, to show how scientific research can provide definitive answers.

• Psychologists: Psychologists can help explain why people tend to believe myths in the first place (e.g., cognitive bias, role of emotions in belief formation, necessity that they are determined in a chaotic world).

2.4 A common pitfall in myth destruction

Despite the best efforts, debunking myths can sometimes be difficult. This section would require:

• Confirmation bias: The tendency of people to accept evidence that supports their existing beliefs and reject evidence to the contrary.

• Cultural and emotional factors: how myth can be intimately tied to cultural identity, making it unacceptable even in the face of hard evidence.

• External Influence: Sometimes, when myths are directly dismissed, people can become deeply entrenched in their beliefs, a psychological phenomenon known as "external influence."

2.5 Limits on myth breaking

Finally, the limitations of myth-breaking should be discussed in this section. A myth is so culturally ingrained or emotionally powerful that it resists disproving it. Others are too vague or difficult to prove. This may include a discussion of:

• Subjective myths: Myths and legends can sometimes be roots of truth or moral lessons that are not easily dismissed.

• The social function of myths: While myths may not always be "true" in the literal sense, they often serve a larger social or cultural purpose, making them difficult to "create".

Chapter 3: The Lost City of Atlantis
Atlantis is An overview of the legend
Describe the myth of Atlantis as told by the ancient Greek philosopher Plato. Discuss his descriptions of Atlantis as a powerful and advanced civilization anchored in the sea.

Where did the story start?
Explain the motivation for storytelling in Plato's dialogues and explain the role of myth in Greek culture.

Thoughts on Atlantis
Summarize the main ideas for the possible location of Atlantis, including the Greek island of Santorini, Donana National Park in Spain, and other possible locations.

Archaeological evidence
Look for evidence (or lack thereof) of underwater archaeology and geology. Discuss the findings that support or prove the existence of Atlantis.

Influence of the Atlantis myth
Discuss how the myth of Atlantis influenced culture, literature, and science fiction, and why the myth persists even without evidence.

Chapter 4: Cleopatra, Queen of the Nile

The legend of Cleopatra
The introduction of Cleopatra VII as the mythical "temptress" and "femme fatale" as portrayed in Roman propaganda and popular media.

Historical context and facts
Present Cleopatra as a highly educated and politically savvy leader, emphasizing her many speeches, treaties and accomplishments.

Roman influence on his character
Discuss how Roman historians, including Plutarch, criticized Cleopatra for portraying her as a dangerous foreigner who threatened Rome.

Archaeological investigations
Detail some archaeological findings that have contributed to our understanding of Cleopatra's reign, including her relationship with Julius Caesar and Mark Antony.

The Legacy of Cleopatra
Analysed the impact of Cleopatra's myth on art, literature, and film, comparing these depictions to her historical image as a ruler.

Chapter 5: Trojan Code
Legend of the Trojan War
The legend of the Trojan War is a Greek myth about a war that began when Paris, the prince of Troy, kidnapped Helen, the wife of King Menelaus of Sparta
Summarize the Iliad and Odyssey, focusing on the concept of famous characters, the Trojan horse, and the Ten Years War against Helen of Troy.
Historical Review of Troy

Describe the 19th century discovery by Heinrich Schliemann of what is believed to be Troy and his archaeological excavations in Turkey.

Did a war really happen?
Explore hypotheses about whether a Trojan War-like conflict occurred, including possible trade disputes, territorial wars, or symbolic repetition

A lie is a separation from reality
Analysis of book presentations and possible historical facts, such as the existence of a large horse system and mythological elements.

Troy cultural influence
Consider the impact of the Trojan War on literature, art, and culture, and why the story takes so long.

Chapter 6: Ancient Wonders and Mysteries

Overview of the Ancient Wonders
Introduce the Seven Wonders of the Ancient World, with a focus on the Great Pyramid of Giza, the Hanging Gardens of Babylon, and the Colossus of Rhodes.

The Great Pyramid of Giza
Examine common myths surrounding the Great Pyramid: from its construction by aliens to hidden chambers and curses.

Provide an overview of modern archaeological evidence about how it was likely built using ingenious engineering techniques.

The Hanging Gardens of Babylon
Discuss the mystery of the Hanging Gardens, including whether they truly existed. Introduce archaeological findings and theories regarding their location.

The Colossus of Rhodes and Other Wonders
Describe the historical records and myths around the Colossus, the Statue of Zeus, and others. Discuss their cultural and architectural significance.

The Legacy of the Seven Wonders
Explore how these Wonders have inspired architecture, engineering, and storytelling throughout history.

Part II Myths in Science

Chapter 7: The 10% Brain Myth
Origins of the Myth
Trace the origins of the claim that "we only use 10% of our brains," attributed to figures like Albert Einstein and misunderstood studies of brain function.

Why the Myth Persists
Examine why this myth is so appealing—its connection to ideas of untapped potential and self-improvement.

Scientific Reality
Present evidence from neuroimaging that shows brain activity across nearly all regions, even during simple tasks.

The Power of Neuroplasticity
Highlight the real capabilities of the brain, including neuroplasticity, to explain how the brain truly grows and adapts.

Impact of the Myth on Culture
Analyse how this myth has influenced self-help books, movies, and beliefs about "hidden potential."

Chapter 8: Evolutionary Myths
Debunking "Missing Link" Misconceptions
Explain the misconception of the "missing link" in human evolution and clarify how evolution is a gradual process with transitional fossils.

Misunderstanding Darwin's Theory
Clarify that Darwin did not say "survival of the fittest" in the way it's often portrayed and explain the true meaning of "natural selection."

Evolutionary Misconceptions
Discuss myths around "humans evolved from monkeys" and clarify the branching nature of evolutionary trees.

The Complexity of Human Evolution
Present recent discoveries that show the complexity of human
evolution, including interbreeding with Neanderthals and Denisovans.
Evolution Myths in Society
Examine how misunderstandings about evolution fuel debates on education, religion, and science denial.

Chapter 9: Space and the Moon Landing Hoax

The Moon Landing Hoax Theory
Introduce the myth that the 1969 moon landing was faked and originated as Cold War propaganda.

Analysing "Evidence" for the Hoax
Address common arguments from conspiracy theorists, such as shadows in photos, the lack of stars, and the waving flag, with scientific explanations for each.

Scientific Evidence of the Moon Landings
Present evidence including moon rocks, Apollo mission
Recordings and the on-going presence of objects left on the moon.

Psychology of Conspiracy Theories
Explore why moon landing myths persist, touching on human psychology, distrust in government, and the appeal of "hidden truths."

The Legacy of the Moon Landing
Reflect on how these myths detract from real scientific achievements and how they're countered by on-going space exploration.

Chapter 10: Common Misunderstandings in Physics
Misconceptions About Black Holes
Explain common myths, like "black holes are cosmic vacuums that suck up everything," and clarify what black holes actually do in space.

The Misunderstood Quantum World
Tackle myths like "quantum physics means we can change reality with our minds" and clarify the real findings of quantum mechanics.

Parallel Universes and Multiverse Myths
Address popular interpretations of parallel universes and multiverses, differentiating scientific theories from science fiction.

Misunderstandings About Relativity
Simplify the basics of Einstein's theory of relativity and address myths like "time travel is possible because of relativity."

Impact of Physics Myths on Popular Culture
Discuss how these myths fuel science fiction but also contribute to public misunderstanding, and how popular science attempts to bridge this gap.

Part III: Myths in Medicine and Health

Chapter 11: Ancient Healing Myths
Origins of Ancient Remedies
Introduce common ancient remedies and healing practices, from bloodletting and leeches to acupuncture and Ayurveda medicine.

Myths and Beliefs Around Ancient Medicine
Discuss the belief that "older" equals "better" when it comes to natural and traditional medicine.

Examining Evidence
Review what modern science says about the effectiveness of certain ancient practices, such as acupuncture and herbal treatments, and clarify where they work and where they fall short.

Placebo Effect in Ancient Remedies

The placebo effect is when a person's health improves after taking a fake or inactive treatment, also known as a placebo. Placebos can be sugar pills, injections of water or saline, or even fake surgical procedures.

The placebo effect is caused by a person's belief in the treatment and their expectation of feeling better, rather than the characteristics of the placebo. Placebos can be powerful and can have an effect on a variety of conditions, including:

Migraines, Joint pain, Arthritis, Asthma, High blood pressure, Depression, Pain, Sleep disorders, Irritable bowel syndrome, and Menopause

Impact on Modern Health Choices
Explore how these myths influence contemporary health practices and the popularity of "natural" treatments. The placebo effect is a real phenomenon, and the idea that it's a myth is a misconception:

Explanation
The placebo effect is when a person experiences a physical benefit from a treatment that doesn't contain an active ingredient, such as a sugar pill. Research shows that placebos can cause measurable physiological changes, similar to those caused by effective medications. For example, a review of cough medication trials found that 85% of the reduction in cough was related to the placebo, not the active ingredient.

Chapter 12: Health Myths That Persist Today
The "8 Glasses of Water" Myth

Explain the origins of the "eight glasses a day" guideline and what modern research suggests about hydration needs. The idea that people should drink eight glasses of water per day is a myth. The actual amount of water a person needs depends on several factors, including their size, what they eat, where they live, and what they're doing

Cold Weather Causes Colds
Explore the common belief that cold weather directly causes illness, and clarify the role of viruses and immune response.

Myths Around "Detoxing" and "Cleansing"
Examine detox diets, juice cleanses, and the belief that the body needs help to "remove toxins," clarifying how the liver and kidneys naturally detoxify the body.

Myths About Sugar and Hyperactivity
Address the belief that sugar causes hyperactivity in children and
review what research says about sugar and behaviour. Multiple studies have found no link between sugar and hyperactivity. In fact, some studies suggest that sugar may have a calming effect.

Misconceptions About "Eating Fat Makes You Fat"
A small amount of healthy fat is necessary for the body to function properly. Healthy fats help the body absorb vitamins, maintain cell membranes, and regulate hormones.
The type of fat you consume is more important than the amount. You should avoid harmful artificial trans fats and choose heart-healthy fats like monounsaturated and polyunsaturated fats from nuts, fish, and plant-based oils.

Chapter 13: Alternative Medicine vs. Science
Overview of Alternative Medicine
Introduce the popularity of alternative treatments like homeopathy, chiropractic care, and herbal medicine, and explain why they attract people.

The Science of Homeopathy
Explain what homeopathy is, the "law of similars," and why homeopathic remedies have little scientific support.

Herbal Medicine Myths
Discuss common beliefs about herbs being "safer" or more

"Natural" than pharmaceuticals and clarify the risks and benefits.
Chiropractic Care and Spinal Manipulation

Examine the myths around chiropractic care's ability to cure a wide range of ailments and provide insights from research on its effectiveness.

The Risks of Alternative Medicine
Explore cases where alternative treatments may interfere with conventional medical care, highlighting the importance of evidence-based medicine.

Chapter 14: Fitness Myths
"No Pain, No Gain"

"No pain, no gain" is a common fitness myth that can lead to injuries and other negative consequences. In reality, exercise should never hurt, and pain is a sign that something is wrong. Here are some things to know about pain and exercise
The idea that you need to experience pain to work out hard is a common fitness myth that should be avoided. In fact, delayed onset muscle soreness (DOMS) is a protective response to new or excessive exercise, and is not an indication of how effective your workout was.
Here are some other common fitness myths:
Spot reduction: It's not possible to choose where to lose fat on your body. The body decides where to burn fat from. However, exercising certain muscles can help tone them and make them look leaner.
The more you sweat, the more calories you burn: This is not true.
Crunches will give you sculpted abs: You can do 100 crunches a day for 100 days and still not see results. Instead, you should focus on a mix of strength training and endurance exercises, and manage your nutrition.
Cardio is the only way to lose weight: This is not true.
Lifting heavy weights will make you bulky: This is not true

Part IV: Natural World Myths

Chapter 15: Animal Myths

Misunderstandings About Wolves

Explore the myth of the "lone wolf" and misconceptions around wolves as dangerous, solitary predators. Present real insights into wolf social structures and behaviour.
In human society, the term "lone wolf" can be used to describe someone who is perceived as eccentric, unsocial, or even threatening.
The myth of the lone wolf in war reporting is the idea that male reporters travel solo around the world in search of the truth. In reality, reporters in war zones are usually embedded in organizations
The myth of the lone wolf in popular culture is the idea that men should be strong and independent, and that they should not need to rely on others

Bats and Vampires

Address myths that associate bats with vampires, disease, and danger. Explain the ecological importance of bats and their role in pest control and pollination.

Snakes and Venom Myths
Discuss common myths that all snakes are deadly or aggressive, clarify the difference between venomous and non-venomous snakes, and describe their role in controlling pest populations.

Owls as Omens
Examine myths around owls as symbols of death or bad luck in various cultures and explore the science of owl behaviour and their benefits to the ecosystem.

Cultural Impact of Animal Myths
Animal myths and folklore have a significant cultural impact in many ways, including:
Passing down cultural wisdom
Animal characters in stories like Aesop's fables and African folklore teach moral lessons and convey cultural values.

Expressing worldview
The relationships between humans, animals, and plants in myths and legends reflect the worldview of a people. For example, the Kalahari San and the Masai have different ways of relating to nature.
Influencing human perception
Cultural aspects influence how humans perceive animals, which can lead to feelings of attraction or repulsion.
Defining how humans use animals
Culture influences how humans use animals, which can lead to attitudes of conservation or persecution.

Chapter 16: Forest and Mountain Myths

There are many myths and legends about forests and mountains, including:
The Himalayas
The home of many gods and goddesses, including Shiva, the Lord of the Himalayas; Parvati, the embodiment of feminine power; and Ganesha, the elephant-headed god who protects travelers.

Mount Kailas
A sacred mountain in Hinduism, where Shiva resides. Buddhists believe that Samvara, a guardian deity, lives on Mount Kailash.
Mount Meru
A cosmic mountain in Indian religions that is the center of all creation. In Hinduism, it is believed that Shiva and Parvati live on Mount Meru.
Himavanta
A legendary forest in the Himalayas that is home to many mythical creatures, including Phaya Naga, Phaya Krut, and Kinnaree.
Wayland Wood
A wood that is said to be haunted by the spirits of two orphaned children who were murdered by their uncle.
The Lost Hill of Faces
A place in Northeast India where a craftsman carved statues of all the gods and goddesses in one night.
Enchanted forests
Forests that are often home to dragons, dwarves, elves, fairies, giants, gnomes, satyrs, goblins, orcs, trolls, dark elves, leprechauns, centaurs, half-elves, and unicorns

Mythical creatures and beings associated with mountains Yetis or Abominable Snowmen –
These legendary creatures are said to live in the Himalayas and other high-altitude regions of
Asia. They are often depicted as large, hairy humanoids who are skilled climbers and can
communicate with animals.
Enchanted Forests and Fairy Tales

Investigate myths about magical or haunted forests, like Germany's Black Forest and Japan's
Aokigahara. Explain the psychological and cultural factors that contribute to these beliefs.

Haunted Mountains
Discuss myths surrounding mountain locations with supernatural reputations, like the Himalayas
and the Ural Mountains. Include stories of strange disappearances and phenomena.

Sacred Mountains and Legends
Examine why certain mountains are considered sacred or magical, such as Mount Olympus,
Machu Picchu, and Mount Kailash. Look into their spiritual significance in various cultures.

Impact of Myths on Environmental Conservation
Discuss how myths sometimes help preserve natural landscapes, as beliefs about sacredness
can protect areas from development.

Chapter 17: Ocean Myths

Mermaids and Underwater Creatures

Dive into the origins of mermaid legends and other mythical sea creatures, like the Kraken and
Leviathan. Discuss the psychological basis of "mermaid sightings" and explain how they might be
linked to marine animals, such as manatees.

The Bermuda Triangle

Explain the myth of the Bermuda Triangle as a dangerous area where ships and planes
mysteriously disappear. Provide scientific explanations for these incidents, including natural
phenomena like
rogue waves and magnetic anomalies.

Myths About Sharks
Dispel myths about sharks being ruthless man-eaters, presenting the actual likelihood of shark
attacks and the ecological importance of sharks in marine ecosystems.

The Mystery of the Loch Ness Monster
Explore the history of Loch Ness monster sightings, potential scientific explanations, and the
impact of modern tourism on Loch Ness.

Influence of Ocean Myths on Exploration and Conservation
analyse how ocean myths influence people's perceptions of the sea and marine life, sometimes
encouraging fear or avoidance but also fascination and protection.

Chapter 18: Weather Myths

"Lightning Never Strikes the Same Place Twice"
Explain this popular myth and the real science behind lightning, including why certain locations
are actually more prone to multiple strikes.

"Tornadoes Avoid Cities"
Dispel the misconception that cities are immune to tornadoes, providing examples of urban tornadoes and explaining factors that influence tornado paths.

Weather Superstitions and Sayings
Examine sayings like "Red sky at night, sailor's delight" and "March comes in like a lion and goes out like a lamb." Explain the origins of these phrases and whether they have any scientific basis.

Myths about Hurricanes and Earthquakes

Explore common misunderstandings about hurricanes (e.g., breaking windows to "equalize pressure") and earthquakes (e.g., animals sensing them in advance). Explain the real science and safety tips.

Climate Change Myths
Address myths related to climate change, including misconceptions about global warming, and clarify the basics of climate science and its impact on weather patterns.

Part V: Cultural and Religious Myths

Chapter 19: Creation Myths across Cultures

Introduction to Creation Myths
Provide an overview of creation myths from different cultures, such as the Hindu creation story, the Christian and Jewish Genesis, the Egyptian creation myths, and the Norse cosmogony.

Symbolism in Creation Stories
Discuss the common themes across creation myths, like chaos to order, water as the origin of life, and divine beings shaping the earth.

Scientific Insights into Origins
Compare these stories with scientific explanations for the universe's origins, such as the Big Bang theory and evolutionary biology.

Why Creation Myths Endure
analyse the cultural significance of creation myths and why societies continue to preserve and honor these origin stories.

Impact on Worldviews
Discuss how creation myths shape cultural values, morality, and views of the natural world.

Chapter 20: Myths of the Afterlife
Varied Visions of the Afterlife

Explore beliefs about the afterlife across cultures, such as the Egyptian underworld, the Hindu concept of reincarnation, and the Norse Valhalla.

Symbolism and Common Themes
Examine recurring themes like judgment, reward and punishment, and the soul's journey after death.

Psychological and Cultural Significance
Discuss how these myths offer comfort, establish moral guidelines, and address human fears about mortality.

Scientific Perspective on Consciousness and Death
Explore what science tells us about consciousness and death, and why these mysteries continue to inspire diverse beliefs about the afterlife.

Influence on Cultural Practices
Look at how afterlife myths influence rituals, burial practices, and mourning traditions worldwide.

Chapter 21: Myths of Good vs. Evil

The Archetype of Good vs. Evil
Introduce the universal theme of good vs. evil, drawing from myths like the Zoroastrian duality of Ahura Mazda and Angra Mainyu, and the Christian battle between God and Satan.

Symbolism in Good vs. Evil Myths
analyse symbols of light vs. darkness, order vs. chaos, and purity vs. corruption in these myths.

Psychological Basis for the Duality
Explore the psychological reasons behind the dichotomy of good and evil and how it helps societies define ethics and morality.

Modern Interpretations
Discuss how good vs. evil myths have evolved in modern culture, influencing films, literature, and popular media.

Impact on Social and Moral Values
Examine how these myths continue to shape cultural and moral values, often influencing laws, social expectations, and personal ethics.

Chapter 22: Hero Myths and Legends
The Hero's Journey Archetype
Present the "hero's journey" as found in myths like Hercules, the Ramayana's Rama, and the Arthurian legends.

Symbolic Elements in Hero Myths
Explore key symbols like the call to adventure, trials, mentors, and the hero's return, and explain how these elements reflect human struggles and triumphs.

Cultural Significance of Hero Myths
Analyse how hero myths inspire people to overcome challenges and aspire to greatness within their own lives.

Modern Heroes and Myths

Discuss how traditional hero myths have influenced modern heroes in movies, books, and public figures.

Psychological Impact on Society
Reflect on how hero myths contribute to a sense of purpose, bravery, and resilience in various cultures.

Chapter 23: Myths of Divine Intervention
Stories of Miracles and Divine Actions
Summarize well-known stories of divine intervention, such as the parting of the Red Sea, the Greek gods influencing battles, and miraculous healings.

Purpose and Symbolism of Divine Intervention
Explain the role of divine intervention as a way to explain the
Unexplainable, reinforce faith, or demonstrate divine power.

Historical Explanations for Miracles
Examine historical and natural explanations for certain events described as miracles, exploring phenomena like volcanic eruptions and weather anomalies.

Role of Divine Intervention in Faith
analyse how the belief in divine intervention strengthens religious devotion and impacts people's faith in times of crisis.

Modern Skepticism and Faith
Discuss how people today balance faith in miracles with scientific skepticism, and the impact this has on religious belief.

Chapter 24: Myths About the End of the World
Apocalyptic Myths Across Cultures
Introduce apocalyptic myths from various cultures, such as the Norse Ragnarok, the Christian Revelation, and the Mayan calendar
prophecy.

Symbolic Meaning of Apocalypse
Discuss the role of end-times myths as a way for societies to explore fears of societal collapse, judgment, and rebirth.

Psychological Impact of Apocalyptic Beliefs
Explore why people are fascinated by apocalyptic predictions, often linked to existential fears and a desire for renewal or justice.

Historical and Scientific Context
Examine how certain apocalyptic myths arose in response to real-world events, like natural disasters or social upheaval, and what science tells us about actual threats to human survival.

Influence on Modern Society
Reflect on how apocalyptic myths shape modern concerns, including environmentalism and survivalist, and why people continue to envision potential world-ending scenarios.

Chapter 6: Technology and Modern Myths

Section 1: AI and Automation Myths

"AI Will Take Over the World"
Explore the myth that AI will develop autonomous, world-dominating intelligence, often fuelled by sci-fi movies and literature. Explain the reality of AI's current limitations, focusing on narrow vs. general AI and the technical challenges in creating superintelligent machines.

"Robots Will Take All Jobs"
Address the widespread fear that automation will result in massive
job loss, exploring which industries are most likely to be affected and the potential for new job creation. Discuss real data on AI's impact on jobs and potential strategies for adapting to a tech-driven job market.

The Myth of "Sentient AI"
Clarify misconceptions about AI achieving consciousness or feelings, explaining how AI models work based on algorithms and data, rather than sentience. Discuss ethical considerations in developing advanced AI.

Section 2: Myths About Privacy and Surveillance
"Big Brother Is Watching Everyone"

Unpack the fear that governments or corporations constantly monitor all aspects of daily life. Explain how data collection actually works, addressing data privacy laws, limitations of surveillance technologies, and real risks of data misuse.

The "Privacy on Social Media" Myth
Examine the myth that people can control their privacy on social media simply through privacy settings. Explain how platforms
track and use personal information, even with privacy controls, and offer insights into managing digital footprints.

Facial Recognition Myths
Discuss misconceptions about facial recognition technology, including beliefs that it's infallible and widely used to monitor the public. Clarify how this technology works, its accuracy issues (e.g., bias in recognition algorithms), and current regulatory debates.

Section 3: Myths Around the Internet and Cyber security

"The Internet Is Anonymous"
Address the myth that people can be truly anonymous online, clarifying what anonymity means and how IP addresses, digital fingerprints, and data trails can still identify users.

The Myth of "Free" Apps and Services
Explain the idea that free apps and platforms are actually funded by user data, often leading to targeted ads or selling data to third parties. Discuss the "nothing is free" concept in digital platforms.
"Hackers Can Easily Steal Anything"

Debunk the myth that hackers can effortlessly breach any system, explaining the realities of cyber security defences and common weak points, like social engineering and phishing. Provide insights on basic steps for protecting digital information.

Section 4: Social Media Myths
"Social Media Reflects Real Life"
analyse the myth that social media accurately reflects people's real lives, explaining the phenomenon of curated and exaggerated online personas. Discuss the psychological effects of comparing oneself to others on social media and how it impacts mental health.

"Going Viral Is Easy"
Address the belief that anyone can quickly go viral, exploring the factors that contribute to viral content, from algorithms to timing. Explain how algorithms work to favour certain types of content and the role of paid promotion.

The Influence of "Influencers" Myth
Examine myths around social media influencers and their actual influence on audiences. Discuss how sponsored content, audience engagement, and brand partnerships shape the influencer industry and how audiences are becoming more sceptical.

Section 5: Myths Surrounding Digital and Virtual Realities

"Virtual Reality (VR) Is Dangerous for Health"
Explore the myth that VR is harmful to eyesight, brain function, or mental health. Clarify known effects, such as VR motion sickness, and discuss precautions for safe VR use.

"The Meta verse Will Replace the Real World"
Address the idea that meta verse technologies (like VR and AR) will eventually lead people to abandon the physical world, explaining the real applications of meta verse tech in gaming, work, and education, and the limitations it currently faces.

"Video Games Cause Violence"
Examine the longstanding belief that violent video games lead to real-life aggression, summarizing what research indicates about
video games and behaviour and debunking the myth based on psychological studies.

Section 6: Space and Technology Myths
"The Moon Landing Was a Hoax"
Debunk one of the most famous conspiracy theories around space technology, presenting the evidence supporting the reality of the moon landings and explaining common misunderstandings that fuel this myth.

"5G and Wireless Technology Are Harmful"
Address fears surrounding 5G, Wi-Fi, and other wireless technologies, clarifying the science behind electromagnetic radiation and health risks and explaining why 5G is no more harmful than previous technologies.

Myths About Space Exploration and Aliens
Explore myths about aliens, UFO sightings, and government cover-ups, providing scientific perspectives on extra-terrestrial life and the limitations of current space technology.

Chapter	Topic	Key Points
Chapter 3	The Lost City of Atlantis	- **Plato's Description**: Atlantis as a powerful, advanced civilization in the sea. - **Story's Origin**: The myth as a part of Plato's dialogues, reflecting Greek cultural views on ideal societies. - **Location Theories**: Possible locations like Santorini, Spain's Donana Park, etc. - **Archaeological Evidence**: Lack of concrete evidence, but on going investigations into underwater sites. - **Cultural Influence**: The myth has influenced literature, art, and sci-fi, persisting despite lack of proof.
Chapter 4	Cleopatra, Queen of the Nile	- **Myth vs. Reality**: Cleopatra as a "temptress" in Roman propaganda vs. her political savvy. - **Historical Facts**: An educated ruler who forged important alliances with Caesar and Antony. - **Roman Influence**: Roman sources, including Plutarch, portrayed her negatively. - **Archaeological Findings**: Excavations revealing her reign, relationships, and political achievements. - **Legacy**: Cleopatra's impact on art, literature, and film contrasts with her real-life political acumen.
Chapter 5	Trojan Code	- **The Trojan War**: Legendary conflict sparked by Paris's abduction of Helen. - **Iliad & Odyssey**: Epic tales focusing on famous characters, the Trojan Horse, and the 10-year war. - **Troy's Discovery**: Schliemann's excavation of ancient Troy in the 19th century. - **Historical Debate**: The possibility of a Trojan War-like conflict—trade wars, territorial disputes, or mythological exaggerations. - **Cultural Influence**: The Trojan War's lasting impact on literature and art.
Chapter 6	Ancient Wonders and Mysteries	- **Seven Wonders Overview**: Focus on the Great Pyramid, Hanging Gardens, and Colossus of Rhodes. - **The Great Pyramid**: Myths of alien construction and hidden chambers; modern archaeological insights. - **Hanging Gardens**: Debate over their existence and location, with evidence pointing to Babylon or Nineveh. - **Colossus and Other Wonders**: Cultural and architectural significance of the Colossus, Statue of Zeus, etc. - **Legacy**: Continued inspiration for architecture, engineering, and storytelling.

Chapter	Topic	Key Points
Chapter 7	The 10% Brain Myth	- **Origins**: The myth that we use only 10% of our brain, often attributed to Einstein and misinterpreted studies. - **Why the Myth Persists**: The appeal of unlocking untapped potential and improving oneself. - **Scientific Reality**: Neuroimaging shows activity across nearly all brain regions during tasks. - **Neuroplasticity**: Real brain power lies in its adaptability and ability to grow. - **Cultural Impact**: The myth has influenced self-help culture, movies, and beliefs in hidden potential.
Chapter 8	Evolutionary Myths	- **Missing Link**: Debunk the "missing link" misconception and explain evolution as a gradual process with transitional fossils. - **Darwin's Theory**: Clarify that Darwin didn't mean "survival of the fittest" as commonly understood; focus on "natural selection." - **Humans and Monkeys**: Address the myth that humans evolved from monkeys; humans and monkeys share common ancestors, not a direct lineage. - **Complexity of Human Evolution**: Recent discoveries show interbreeding with Neanderthals and Denisovans. - **Evolution in Society**: Discuss how evolutionary myths fuel debates about education, religion, and science denial.
Chapter 9	Space and the Moon Landing Hoax	- **Moon Landing Hoax**: Introduce the myth that the 1969 moon landing was faked as Cold War propaganda. - **Analysing Evidence**: Debunk conspiracy theories about photos, shadows, flag movements, and other "evidence" using scientific explanations. - **Scientific Evidence**: Present proof from moon rocks, Apollo mission recordings, and objects still on the moon. - **Psychology of Conspiracy Theories**: Examine why people believe in the hoax, touching on distrust in government and the allure of hidden truths. - **Legacy**: Discuss how the myth undermines real scientific achievements and how space exploration

		counters these myths.
Chapter 10	Common Misunderstandings in Physics	- **Black Holes**: Dispel the myth that black holes are "vacuum cleaners" that suck up everything; explain that they are regions of intense gravity. - **Quantum World**: Clarify the myth that quantum physics allows us to change reality with our minds; discuss real quantum mechanics findings. - **Parallel Universes/Multiverses**: Differentiate between scientific theories about parallel universes and the science fiction interpretation of multiverses. - **Relativity**: Simplify Einstein's theory of relativity, addressing myths like "time travel is possible" due to relativity. - **Cultural Impact**: Discuss how these myths fuel science fiction but also contribute to misunderstandings of science, and how popular science bridges the gap.

Chapter	Topic	Key Points
Chapter 11	Ancient Healing Myths	- **Origins of Ancient Remedies**: Discuss remedies like bloodletting, leeches, acupuncture, and Ayurvedic medicine. - **Myths Around Ancient Medicine**: The belief that older, traditional practices are inherently better. - **Examining Evidence**: Evaluate modern science on the effectiveness of ancient treatments like acupuncture and herbal medicine. - **Placebo Effect**: Explain how placebos (inactive treatments) can cause real health benefits due to belief and expectation. - **Impact on Modern Health Choices**: Explore how ancient healing myths shape contemporary trends in "natural" treatments and alternative health practices.
Chapter 12	Health Myths That Persist Today	- **8 Glasses of Water Myth**: Explain the origin of the "8 glasses per day" guideline and clarify that hydration needs vary by individual. - **Cold Weather and Colds**: Discuss the myth that cold

		weather directly causes colds; the real cause is viruses, not temperature.
		- **Detoxing Myths**: Debunk the idea that the body needs detox diets or juice cleanses; explain how the liver and kidneys naturally detoxify. - **Sugar and Hyperactivity**: Dispel the myth that sugar causes hyperactivity in children; research shows no link, and some studies suggest sugar may have a calming effect. - **Eating Fat Makes You Fat**: Clarify that healthy fats are necessary for body function; the type of fat (not the amount) is key, and healthy fats support various body functions.
Chapter 13	Alternative Medicine vs. Science	- **Overview of Alternative Medicine**: Examine the growing popularity of alternative treatments like homeopathy, chiropractic care, and herbal medicine. - **The Science of Homeopathy**: Explain the principles of homeopathy (law of similars) and its lack of scientific support. - **Herbal Medicine Myths**: Address the belief that herbal remedies are always safer than pharmaceuticals; clarify the risks and benefits. - **Chiropractic Care**: Examine myths around chiropractic care's ability to cure a range of ailments and present evidence on its effectiveness. - **Risks of Alternative Medicine**: Discuss the dangers of relying on alternative treatments instead of evidence-based medicine, including how they may interfere with conventional care.
Chapter 14	Fitness Myths	- **No Pain, No Gain**: Dispel the myth that pain is necessary for effective exercise; pain indicates injury, not progress. - **Spot Reduction**: Clarify that it's impossible to target fat loss in specific areas; fat loss occurs throughout the body. - **Sweating and Calories**: Debunk the myth that sweating equals more calories burned; sweat is a cooling mechanism, not a fat-burning indicator. - **Crunches for Abs**: Explain that crunches alone won't give sculpted abs; a mix of strength training, endurance exercises, and proper nutrition is key. - **Cardio for Weight Loss**: Debunk the idea that cardio is the only way to lose weight; strength training is also crucial. - **Lifting Weights Makes You Bulky**: Dispel the myth that weight lifting leads to bulkiness, emphasizing that it helps build strength without necessarily increasing size.

Chapter	Topic	Details	Key Points
15: Animal Myths	Misunderstandings About Wolves	- Myth of the "lone wolf" as solitary, dangerous.	- Wolves are social animals with strong pack dynamics. - Misuse in media/culture: war reporting, individualism.
	Bats and Vampires	- Bats linked to vampires, danger, and disease.	- Ecological role: pest control, pollination. - Myths overshadow their benefits.
	Snakes and Venom Myths	- Belief that all snakes are deadly or aggressive.	- Venomous ≠ non-venomous. - Role in pest control.
	Owls as Omens	- Owls seen as omens of death or bad luck in some cultures.	- Science: nocturnal hunters aiding ecosystems. - Cultural symbolism varies.
	Cultural Impact of Animal Myths	- Influence on culture, human perception, and conservation efforts.	- Teach lessons (e.g., fables). - Reflect worldviews (e.g., San vs. Masai). - Shape attitudes toward animals.
16: Forest and Mountain Myths	The Himalayas	- Home of Shiva, Parvati, and Ganesha.	- Spiritual and cultural significance.
	Mount Kailash	- Sacred in Hinduism and Buddhism.	- Associated with deities Shiva and Samvara.
	Mount Meru	- Central cosmic mountain in Indian religions.	- Mythical home of divine beings.
	Enchanted Forests	- Forests like Himavanta, Black Forest, and Aokigahara believed to house mythical beings.	- Cultural and psychological roots.
	Haunted Mountains	- Stories of supernatural occurrences (e.g., Himalayas, Ural Mountains).	- Linked to disappearances and myths of the unknown.
	Sacred Mountains	- Examples: Mount Olympus, Machu Picchu, Mount Kailash.	- Revered for spiritual or cultural reasons.
	Impact on Conservation	- Myths help protect natural sites by discouraging exploitation.	- Sacred status aids conservation.
17: Ocean Myths	Mermaids and Underwater Creatures	- Legends of mermaids, Krakens, Leviathans.	- Likely based on manatee sightings. - Fascination with marine life.
	Bermuda Triangle	- Myth of mysterious	- Scientific reasons:

		disappearances.	rogue waves, magnetic anomalies.
	Myths About Sharks	- Sharks wrongly perceived as man-eaters.	- Shark attacks are rare. - Sharks are crucial for marine ecosystems.
	Loch Ness Monster	- Persistent legend tied to Loch Ness.	- Potential explanations: hoaxes, misidentified animals. - Tourism impact.
	Impact on Conservation	- Myths fuel both fear and fascination of the ocean.	- Myths inspire marine protection and exploration.
18: Weather Myths	**Lightning Never Strikes Twice**	- Misconception that lightning avoids the same spot.	- Science: high structures attract repeated strikes.
	Tornadoes Avoid Cities	- Belief that urban areas are immune to tornadoes.	- Examples of urban tornadoes dispel this myth.
	Weather Superstitions	- Sayings like "Red sky at night, sailor's delight."	- Mixed accuracy, often based on regional patterns.
	Hurricanes and Earthquakes	- Misconceptions (e.g., breaking windows for hurricanes, animals sensing quakes).	- Science provides practical safety measures.
	Climate Change Myths	- Misunderstandings about global warming.	- Climate change impacts weather patterns. - Need for accurate scientific understanding.

Chapter	Topic	Details	Key Points
19: Creation Myths	**Introduction to Creation Myths**	Overview of creation stories from cultures like Hindu, Christian, Egyptian, and Norse.	- Diverse interpretations of origins.
	Symbolism in Creation Stories	Common themes like chaos to order, water as life's origin, and divine creation.	- Symbolic patterns reflect cultural values.
	Scientific Insights	Big Bang theory and evolution compared to creation myths.	- Myths vs. scientific explanations.
	Why Creation Myths Endure	Cultural significance and enduring relevance of origin	- Help preserve identity and values.

		stories.	
	Impact on Worldviews	Influence on cultural morality, values, and perception of nature.	- Creation stories define societal outlook.
20: Myths of the Afterlife	Varied Visions of the Afterlife	Afterlife beliefs across cultures: Egyptian underworld, Hindu reincarnation, Norse Valhalla.	- Reflect diverse spiritual perspectives.
	Symbolism and Themes	Judgment, reward/punishment, soul's journey after death.	- Common elements in afterlife myths.
	Psychological and Cultural Significance	Comfort, moral structure, and coping with mortality.	- Address fears of death and provide guidance.
	Scientific Perspectives	Consciousness and death studied scientifically but remain mysteries.	- Myths bridge gaps in understanding.
	Cultural Practices	Influence on rituals, burials, and mourning traditions.	- Practices reflect beliefs in the afterlife.
21: Myths of Good vs. Evil	The Archetype	Universal duality of good vs. evil in myths like Zoroastrian and Christian stories.	- Helps define ethical frameworks.
	Symbolism in Myths	Light vs. darkness, order vs. chaos, purity vs. corruption.	- Symbolic representations of morality.
	Psychological Basis	Explains human need for ethical duality to define social norms.	- Reinforces societal rules and justice.
	Modern Interpretations	Good vs. evil themes in films, literature, and media.	- Myths evolve with culture and technology.
	Impact on Social Values	Influence on laws, social behavior, and personal ethics.	- Shapes moral principles across societies.
22: Hero Myths	The Hero's Journey Archetype	Myths like Hercules, Rama, and Arthur.	- Heroes' struggles and triumphs mirror human experience.
	Symbolism in Hero Myths	Call to adventure, trials, mentors, hero's return.	- Reflect personal growth and resilience.
	Cultural Significance	Inspire individuals to face challenges and achieve greatness.	- Heroes serve as cultural role models.
	Modern Heroes	Traditional myths influence contemporary storytelling and public figures.	- Old archetypes adapted to modern narratives.
	Psychological Impact	Instills purpose, bravery, and societal resilience.	- Heroes encourage collective and individual hope.
23: Myths of Divine Intervention	Stories of Miracles	Examples like the Red Sea parting, Greek gods in battles, miraculous healings.	- Demonstrate divine power and intervention.
	Purpose and Symbolism	Explains the unexplainable, reinforces faith, showcases divine will.	- Strengthens religious devotion.

	Historical Explanations	Events like volcanic eruptions, weather phenomena explained naturally.	- Myths rooted in historical or natural events.
	Role in Faith	Divine interventions boost faith during crises.	- Provides spiritual reassurance.
	Modern Skepticism	Balancing faith in miracles with scientific skepticism.	- Faith and rationality coexist in modern beliefs.
24: End-of-the-World Myths	Apocalyptic Myths	Cultural myths: Norse Ragnarok, Christian Revelation, Mayan calendar prophecy.	- Reflect fears of judgment and rebirth.
	Symbolism of Apocalypse	Explores themes of societal collapse, renewal, justice.	- Explains cycles of destruction and creation.
	Psychological Impact	Fascination tied to existential fears and hope for renewal.	- Myths provide meaning to inevitable ends.
	Historical and Scientific Context	Arise from natural disasters, social crises; science informs real threats.	- Myths contextualize historical phenomena.
	Influence on Modern Society	Shaping environmentalism, survivalist culture, and end-of-world scenarios.	- Drives awareness of existential threats and solutions.

Section	Myth	Key Details	Insights
1: AI and Automation Myths	AI Will Take Over the World	Sci-fi fuels fears of superintelligent AI domination. Current AI is narrow and task-specific, with general AI far from reality.	- AI's limitations show no immediate risk of global control.
	Robots Will Take All Jobs	Fears of massive job loss due to automation. Certain industries are more impacted, but tech creates new roles.	- Adapting skills and policies is crucial for tech-driven economies.
	The Myth of Sentient AI	Misconceptions about AI consciousness; AI works through algorithms and data without emotions.	- AI is advanced but not self-aware. Ethical considerations remain vital.
2: Privacy and Surveillance	Big Brother Is Watching Everyone	Fear of constant surveillance by governments/corporations. Data collection is regulated and not as pervasive as imagined but still poses risks.	- Transparency and better privacy policies needed to ensure trust.
	Privacy on Social Media	Misconception that privacy settings guarantee online security. Platforms track data beyond user control.	- Managing digital footprints requires vigilance and informed choices.
	Facial	Beliefs in infallibility and pervasive	- Technology must

	Recognition Myths	use. Reality includes biases, accuracy issues, and evolving regulations.	address ethical and technical challenges.
3: Internet and Cybersecurity Myths	The Internet Is Anonymous	True anonymity is rare; IP addresses and data trails often identify users.	- Understanding digital footprints is key to online safety.
	The Myth of "Free" Apps	Free platforms monetize user data, often leading to targeted ads or third-party sales.	- "Nothing is free" applies strongly to digital services.
	Hackers Can Easily Steal Anything	Hacking depends on exploiting weak points like phishing; strong cybersecurity measures can deter breaches.	- Awareness and basic precautions can significantly reduce risks.
4: Social Media Myths	Social Media Reflects Real Life	Social media shows curated and exaggerated personas, distorting reality.	- Comparing oneself to others online can harm mental health.
	Going Viral Is Easy	Viral content is influenced by algorithms, timing, and often paid promotion.	- Virality is rare and often strategically orchestrated.
	The Influence of Influencers	Myths about influencers' impact; audience engagement and sponsored content shape perceptions.	- Audiences are becoming more skeptical of influencer authenticity.
5: Digital and Virtual Realities Myths	VR Is Dangerous for Health	Concerns about eyesight, brain function, and mental health. VR motion sickness is real but manageable with precautions.	- VR is generally safe with proper usage.
	The Metaverse Will Replace Real Life	Myth that AR/VR will cause detachment from the physical world. Real uses include gaming, education, and work, but tech faces many limitations.	- Metaverse tech complements rather than replaces real-world interactions.
	Video Games Cause Violence	Misconceptions about gaming and aggression; research shows no direct link between violent games and real-life violence.	- Psychological studies debunk this myth, showing games are not inherently harmful.
6: Space and Technology Myths	The Moon Landing Was a Hoax	Popular conspiracy debunked through evidence like telemetry data, samples, and global observation.	- Science and transparency counter conspiracy theories.
	5G and Wireless Tech Are Harmful	Fears about health risks debunked through scientific evidence; electromagnetic radiation levels in 5G are non-threatening.	- Public education needed to dispel misinformation.
	Myths About Space Exploration & Aliens	Alien myths fueled by UFO sightings and government secrecy; scientific exploration focuses on exoplanets and advanced signal detection.	- Current space tech is limited, but ongoing research explores the potential for extraterrestrial life.

Conclusion

Conclusion: Beyond Myths – Embracing Truth and Understanding

In exploring the myths that weave through history, culture, science, medicine, nature, and technology, we have encountered a fascinating blend of stories that reveal the rich tapestry of human belief. From ancient creation tales to modern technological misconceptions, myths serve as mirrors reflecting humanity's deepest fears, aspirations, and mysteries. They offer insight into how societies understand their world, provide comfort in the face of the unknown, and sometimes even foster a shared cultural identity.

Why Myths Endure

Myths endure not simply because they are persistent or widespread but because they fill essential roles in human experience. They provide answers where knowledge is scarce, reinforce social bonds, and help people find meaning. As we have seen, certain myths also arise from understandable misinterpretations of phenomena, from natural events like eclipses to technological advances like artificial intelligence.

Myths may provide temporary explanations or comfort, but unchecked, they can also lead to misunderstandings, unfounded fears, and in some cases, even harm. The belief that vaccines cause autism, for instance, has impacted public health worldwide,
while myths about wildlife can hinder conservation efforts. Recognizing the myths that shape our beliefs is a crucial step toward ensuring we make informed decisions, grounded in evidence rather than fear or misinformation.

The Power of Seeking Truth

In each chapter, we've examined myths through the lenses of history, culture, and science, showing how critical thinking and curiosity can clarify misunderstandings. Embracing truth doesn't mean discarding the value of myths entirely; rather, it means balancing tradition with evidence. When we question and investigate, we don't lose the magic of wonder—instead, we gain a more profound appreciation for the world as it truly is. Understanding that lightning can indeed strike the same place twice, for instance, or that AI is not poised to "take over," empowers us to approach life with realism and responsibility.

Moving Forward with an Informed Perspective

In the modern world, we are surrounded by information—some of it accurate, some of it deceptive. The ability to distinguish between fact and fiction is an essential skill. As we part with some of the myths covered here, we gain a clearer lens for viewing new ones that may arise, especially as science and technology continue to evolve. Whether navigating the latest news about health breakthroughs, technological advances, or environmental changes, this book's journey has shown the importance of seeking truth as a foundation for wise decisions.

Embracing Both Wonder and Knowledge

This exploration leaves us not in a world devoid of wonder but in one where knowledge enhances curiosity. The moon landing may be grounded in fact rather than conspiracy, but it is no less awe-
inspiring. The intricate neural networks powering AI are not conscious, yet they are still extraordinary achievements of human ingenuity. By separating myth from reality, we honour both the human need for stories and the importance of truth.

In conclusion, myths reflect our complex relationship with the world, an interplay of imagination and reality. May this journey inspire you to question, explore, and celebrate the real mysteries of life with curiosity and an open mind. When we embrace both wonder and wisdom, we walk a path that respects the beauty of our myths while grounded in the transformative power of truth.

End Disclaimer

The content in this book is intended for informational and educational purposes. While every effort has been made to ensure the accuracy of the information, this book does not claim to be an exhaustive or definitive source on all myths and beliefs. The interpretations and perspectives offered here reflect careful research and aim to provide readers with insights into historical, cultural, scientific, and technological viewpoints. However, readers are encouraged to approach these subjects critically and to explore further resources if they wish to deepen their understanding.

Cultural Sensitivity: Many of the topics in this book relate to long-standing cultural and religious beliefs, which are deeply personal and significant to individuals and communities. It is not the intention of this book to dismiss or discredit these beliefs. Rather, this exploration seeks to provide context, highlight historical and scientific perspectives, and encourage an informed dialogue on commonly held myths. Readers are invited to engage with these discussions respectfully, bearing in mind that the intent is to foster understanding, not to challenge personal faith or cultural identity.

Author's Confession

> Writing about myths—especially those rooted in culture, religion, and science—has been both a privilege and a challenge. As an author, I approach this topic with great respect for the countless traditions, beliefs, and stories that form the heart of human experience. I am acutely aware that myths serve many roles: they inspire, offer comfort, provide guidance, and define identities. In some cases, myths even reveal truths about human nature that factual accounts may miss.

I must confess that this journey has challenged my own beliefs and assumptions. While researching and writing, I found myself humbled by the complexity of these myths and the insights they offer into human psychology and culture. Although my goal has been to bring clarity and foster critical thinking, I recognize that not all readers will share my interpretations. This book is not an attempt to claim absolute knowledge or to "debunk" cherished
Beliefs but rather to invite readers to consider alternative perspectives.

There may be gaps or oversights in this book, as myths are vast and interpretations can vary widely. I invite readers to view this as a starting point—a way to spark curiosity, encourages questioning, and inspire further exploration. My hope is that this book will open doors to new understandings while honouring the deep significance that myths hold in our collective consciousness.

www.ingramcontent.com/pod-product-compliance
Lightning Source LLC
Chambersburg PA
CBHW072343270726
48659CB00023B/2359